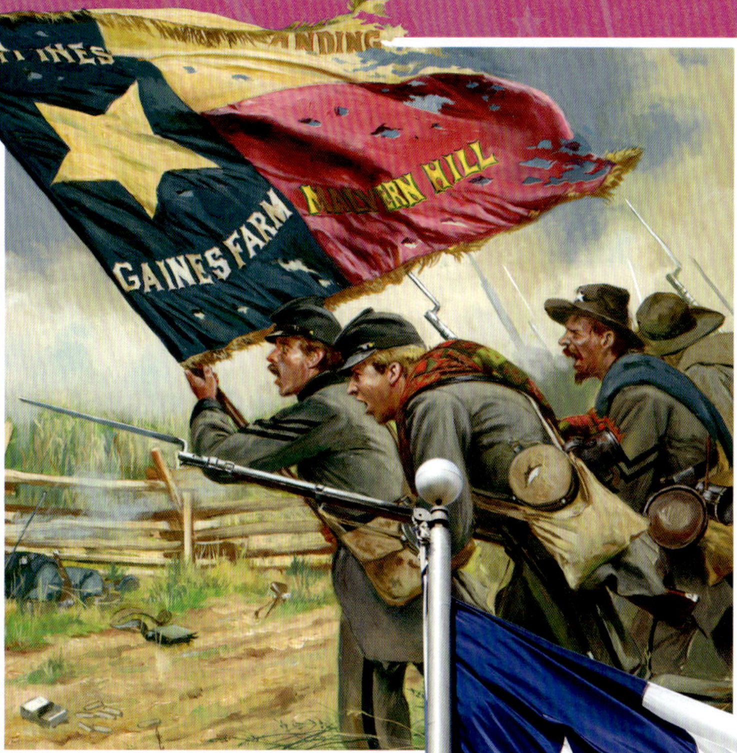

SYMBOLS OF THE UNITED STATES

Texas Flag

AV2

www.openlightbox.com

Linda Hopkins

Step 1
Go to **www.openlightbox.com**

Step 2
Enter this unique code
YNVIDILZG

Step 3
Explore your interactive eBook!

AV2 is optimized for use on any device

Your interactive eBook comes with...

- **Audio** Listen to the entire book read aloud
- **Videos** Watch informative video clips
- **Weblinks** Gain additional information for research
- **Try This!** Complete activities and hands-on experiments
- **Key Words** Study vocabulary, and complete a matching word activity
- **Quizzes** Test your knowledge
- **Slideshows** View images and captions
- **Share** Share titles within your Learning Management System (LMS) or Library Circulation System
- **Citation** Create bibliographical references following APA, CMOS, and MLA styles

This title is part of our AV2 digital subscription

1-Year Texas Subscription
ISBN 978-1-5105-8659-8

Access hundreds of AV2 titles with our digital subscription.
Sign up for a FREE trial at **www.openlightbox.com/trial**

The digital components of this book are guaranteed to stay active for at least five years from the date of publication.

SYMBOLS OF THE UNITED STATES

Texas Flag

CONTENTS

A STATE FLAG

A flag can be used as a symbol of a country or state.

The Texas flag represents the state of Texas.

The **largest Texas flag** is **100 feet wide** and **150 feet long.**

REPUBLIC OF TEXAS

Texas became its own country in 1836.

Its first flag was blue with a yellow star in the middle.

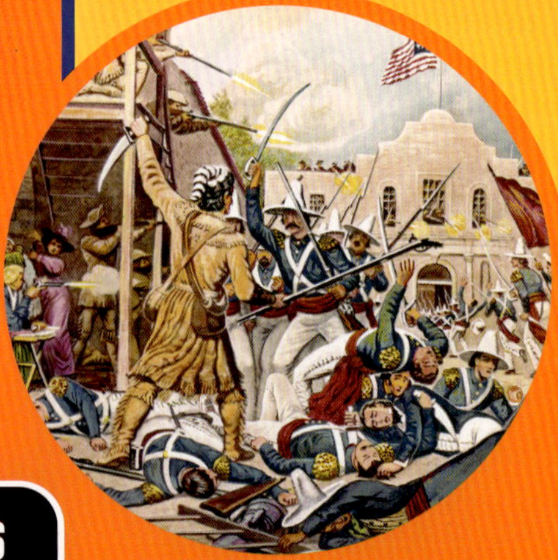

Texas won its independence from Mexico after the **Texas Revolution**, fought from **October 1835** to **April 1836**.

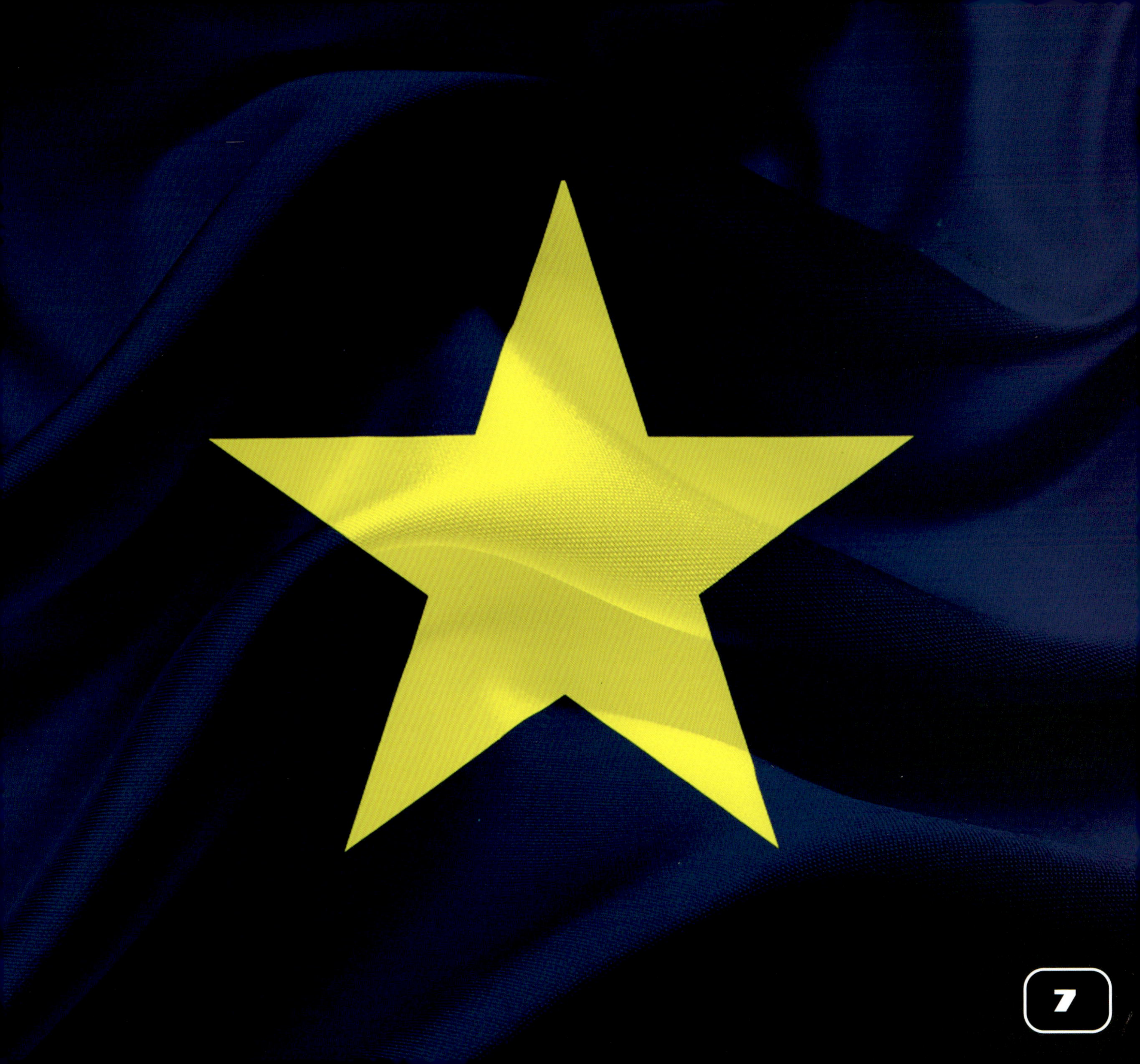

LONE STAR FLAG

In 1839, the Republic of Texas changed its flag to the Lone Star Flag.

This flag is still flown today.

COLORS HAVE MEANING

The Lone Star Flag has three stripes in different colors.

Blue stands for loyalty, and white means purity. Red represents bravery.

PURITY
LOYALTY
BRAVERY

LONE STAR OF TEXAS

There is a single white star on the Texas flag.

This star represents the state's unity.

Texas became the **28th U.S. state** in 1845.

FIVE-POINTED STAR

Each of the five points on the lone star stands for a value.

These values are important to being a good Texan.

LOYALTY
FORTITUDE
RIGHTEOUSNESS
BROADMINDEDNESS
PRUDENCE

"HONOR THE TEXAS FLAG"

Texans say a pledge of allegiance to their flag.

"Honor the Texas flag;
I pledge allegiance to thee,
Texas, one state under God,
one and indivisible."

RESPECTING THE FLAG

People remove their hats before saying the pledge.

They place their right hand over their heart.

THE FLAG TODAY

People in Texas are very proud of the Lone Star Flag.

It is flown beside the U.S. flag across the state.

Texas is sometimes called the **"Lone Star State."**

TEXAS FLAG FACTS

These pages provide detailed information that expands on the interesting facts found in the book. They are intended to be used by adults as a learning support to help young readers round out their knowledge of each icon in the *Symbols of the United States* series.

Pages 4–5

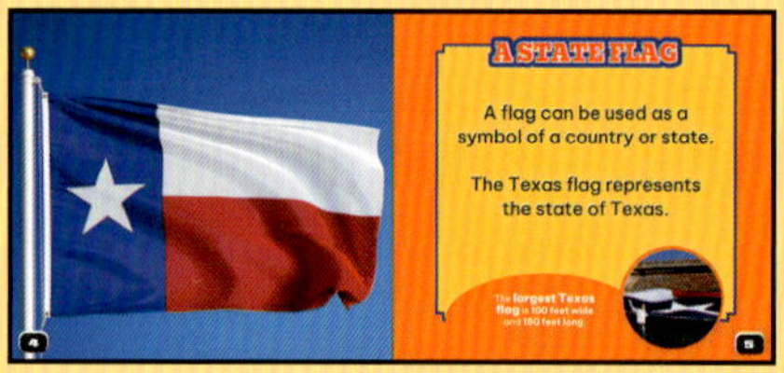

A State Flag

Most flags are made out of cloth and fly on a flagpole, or staff. National flags, such as the U.S. flag, are used to represent countries. State flags represent individual states within countries. Sometimes, a flag is flown at half-mast, or half-staff. This is done to show respect or as a sign of mourning.

Pages 6–7

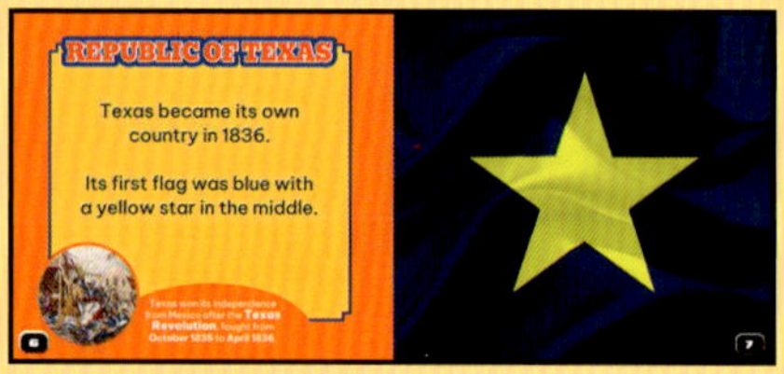

Republic of Texas

Before Texas gained its independence, it was part of Mexico. The Texas Revolution, fought between Mexico and Texas from October 1835 to April 1836, led to the formation of the Republic of Texas. Many notable battles were fought as part of the revolution, including the Battle of the Alamo. Texas declared itself an independent country on March 2, 1836, and was self-governed until it became part of the United States on December 29, 1845.

Pages 8–9

Lone Star Flag

The Lone Star Flag was the official flag of Texas from 1839 to 1879. Between 1879 and 1933, Texas did not have an official flag, although the Lone Star remained popular. In 1933, Texas adopted the Lone Star Flag as its state flag once again. It remains the state's official flag to this day.

Pages 10–11

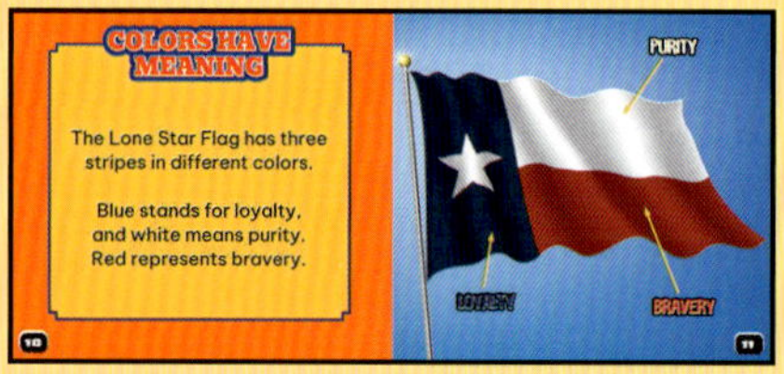

Colors Have Meaning

Texas flies the same red, white, and blue colors as the U.S. flag to show the state's connection to the United States. The Lone Star Flag is notable for its single white star, which is at the center of a vertical blue stripe. This stripe is one-third the length of the flag, and its color represents loyalty. The flag also has two horizontal stripes that are equal in length and width. The stripe on top is white, symbolizing purity. The bottom stripe is red and stands for bravery.

Pages 12–13

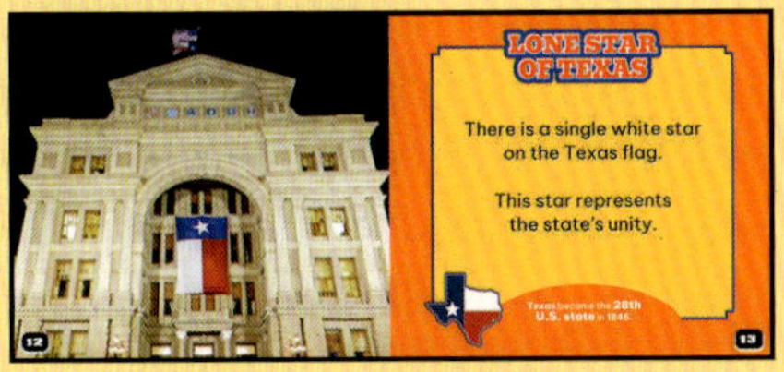

Lone Star of Texas

The single white star, or lone star, on the Texas flag represents the unity of the people of Texas and their struggle for independence. It is also a reminder that Texas was once its own republic. Texas is popularly known as the "Lone Star State."

Pages 14–15

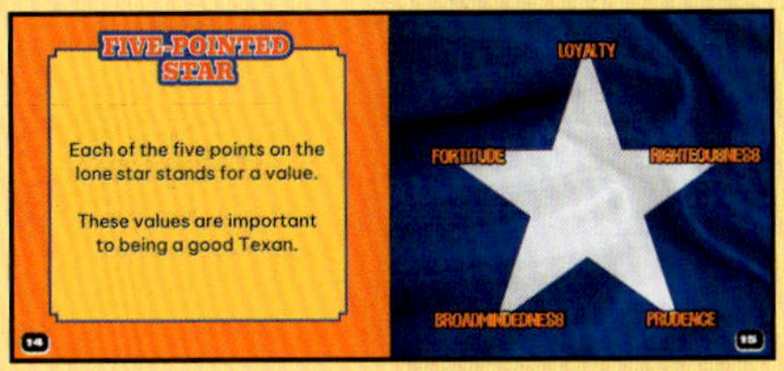

Five-Pointed Star

The lone star of Texas has five points. One of the star's points must point directly upward. Each point stands for a trait or characteristic that a good Texan should possess. The five characteristics represented are fortitude, loyalty, righteousness, prudence, and broadmindedness.

Pages 16–17

"Honor the Texas Flag"

Texas has had a pledge of allegiance to the Lone Star Flag since 1933. Today, students often say it in schools across Texas, along with the pledge of allegiance to the national flag. The Texas pledge of allegiance reads, "Honor the Texas flag; I pledge allegiance to thee, Texas, one state under God, one and indivisible." The pledge of allegiance to the U.S. flag is recited before the pledge to the Texas flag.

Pages 18–19

Respecting the Flag

When reciting the pledge of allegiance to the flag, there are certain customs to follow as a sign of respect. People should always face the flag and remove all head coverings. They place their right hand over their heart, with the fingers touching the left shoulder. The recital of the pledge is followed by a few moments of silence.

Pages 20–21

The Flag Today

Pride in the Lone Star Flag is very evident in Texas. It is often displayed at schools, homes, and businesses throughout the state, and is flown alongside the U.S. flag. The Texas Government Code outlines rules regarding the proper methods of displaying the flag, including when it should be flown at half-staff and full-staff.

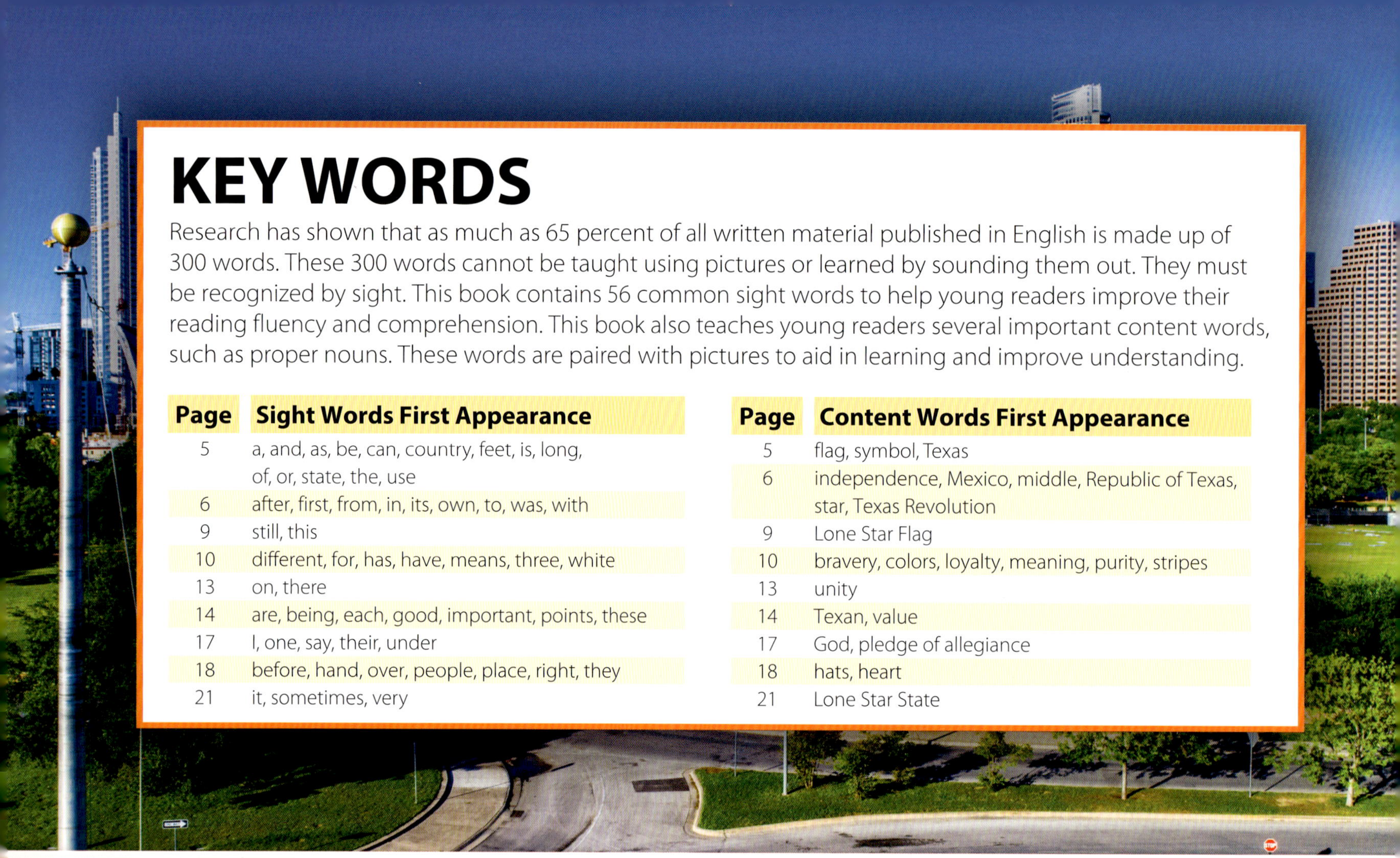

KEY WORDS

Research has shown that as much as 65 percent of all written material published in English is made up of 300 words. These 300 words cannot be taught using pictures or learned by sounding them out. They must be recognized by sight. This book contains 56 common sight words to help young readers improve their reading fluency and comprehension. This book also teaches young readers several important content words, such as proper nouns. These words are paired with pictures to aid in learning and improve understanding.

Page	Sight Words First Appearance
5	a, and, as, be, can, country, feet, is, long, of, or, state, the, use
6	after, first, from, in, its, own, to, was, with
9	still, this
10	different, for, has, have, means, three, white
13	on, there
14	are, being, each, good, important, points, these
17	I, one, say, their, under
18	before, hand, over, people, place, right, they
21	it, sometimes, very

Page	Content Words First Appearance
5	flag, symbol, Texas
6	independence, Mexico, middle, Republic of Texas, star, Texas Revolution
9	Lone Star Flag
10	bravery, colors, loyalty, meaning, purity, stripes
13	unity
14	Texan, value
17	God, pledge of allegiance
18	hats, heart
21	Lone Star State

Published by Lightbox Learning Inc.
276 5th Avenue, Suite 704 #917
New York, NY 10001
Website: www.openlightbox.com

Library of Congress Control Number: 2024938979

ISBN 978-1-5105-8122-7 (hardcover)
ISBN 979-8-8745-1488-4 (softcover)
ISBN 978-1-5105-8287-3 (static multi-user eBook)
ISBN 978-1-5105-8289-7 (interactive multi-user eBook)

Printed in Guangzhou, China
1 2 3 4 5 6 7 8 9 0 28 27 26 25 24

072024
100923

Project Coordinator: Priyanka Das
Designer: Terry Paulhus
Layout: Jean Faye Rodriguez

Every reasonable effort has been made to trace ownership and to obtain permission to reprint copyright material. The publisher would be pleased to have any errors or omissions brought to its attention so that they may be corrected in subsequent printings.

The publisher acknowledges Alamy, Bridgeman Images, Getty Images, and Shutterstock as the primary image suppliers for this title.